INLAND EMPIRE

Poems

by Bradley Brown

Published by:
Dead Poem House
P.O. Box 12685
San Diego, CA 92112

Inland Empire / Poems by Bradley Brown. First Edition. ISBN 9781090627971

For Deborah

Table of Contents

Inland Empire

'Cast out this wicked dream that has seized my heart.'

Teenage Wasteland

She once played me a song
over the phone, set the needle
on the record and

held the receiver to the speaker
I heard the Who's black vinyl
crackle and spin, crackle and spin

Then it was lights out
Windows squeaked
a bed creaked

Getting dressed we talked about its
mountain playground and
cemetery in the sky

Where we would marry
have a darling family
her dream nursery

One night out a week
perhaps an island destination
our dazzling life as committed adults

Until then I waited alone
pounded a bottle on the roof
spun it on the floor

Bradley Brown

Shelf Life

Things got old quick
hide the tear drops
Time to parole, say hello to the ladies
and pardon my French

Goodbye bunkie
my cellie, *mon frere*
Goodbye city of men
dumb library of dick jokes

To you-know-who in Berlin:
mein schnauzer, my road dog
Thank you for showing me how to lift
my leg… and arms attached to fists

Auf wiedersehen set-trippers
and shot-calling swastika boys
that guy with the illegal mustache
would have loved to have your life

Goodbye freaky fascist bastards
goodbye sickos so-called straights
May your eyes be filled with endless vistas
(of cock and anus and hairy balls)

This is goodbye peter gazers and sleight of hand
knuckle-head politicians. Not a good time goon squad

keep the little green men with big black sticks
their money shots, wallet-sized mug shots

Down goes manmade eggs, cups of trickery
Done with hall of mess, time of chow
handouts of packaged mystery meat
and bruised apple pruno shots

As for the pepper spray, no shanks
only perishable items in my state locker
Petty ass bastards, 602 your way back
to the six circles of hell

From an eternity in a level one facility
to some happy hour
full of horny little devils
Cheers to a hot mess

Take me off this cheap display
my date has expired
excusez-moi, time inside
c'est au revoir

Bradley Brown

Exhumation of the Living

I.
Breaths visible
my mom and neighbors
tumble their keys into mumbling locks

They proceed before sunrise
heads lowered, otherworldly silence
curse at no one

Get into a car and shrink into oblivion
distant skylines, wandering buildings
then reappear at evening

slightly disheveled, eyes glaring
carrying bags of dull objects
definitely older

II.
Summer school is the coolest
mixing drinks at your parent's bar, stirring
them with our middle finger, laying

bare flesh on beach towels by the hot tub, playing
very important pop music, and coughing
up smoke as we study

Fall is punishment for more bad grades
I rake dead leaves into a ratty garbage can

the community college in my background

Catch me in the empty garage where echoes are heard
good place to chill when mean sentences come to mind
and I don't want to fight

III.
Will move out next semester, swear on it
Nothing to do except celebrate like a gentleman
stumble across carpet and vomit in bushes

Shadowbox the walls at midnight otherwise
taking jabs at the shrunken head, hanging skeleton
crack in the mirror

Eventually we'll get our own place
throw massive parties to pay the rent
be not so bored to death

There's a bad moon on the ghetto blaster
find something in the ashtray
laugh till we can't breathe

IV.
Got a last minute telephone call
friends of a friend are having friends over
their parents departed for paradise

The body we buried in the sand
at the Spring Break beach party

Bradley Brown

will be there, back for holidays

She wants to hang in a dark field
and will bring friends with her
of a higher class and shorter skirt

First the liquor store where we saw Elvis
they'll sell to anyone with a fake I.D.
No deposit no return

V.
The sun dips into the suburbs
digs us from our slumbers, dusts sleep from our eyes
pulling us outside (and through windows)

Meet a girl at the record store
who likes the same rock star lifestyle
New group, different clothes. Do it all over again

An undertaking for a graduation speech
this wild ride through the halls of academia
Raise the spirit before chasing her shadow

tonight we drink for dead artists, dig their life
New pair of shoes and favorite shirt don't fail me now
there's gonna be a line out the door to sign my yearbook

Have a bitchin' summer
Stay cool
Don't change

This World Naked

Predawn jumpsuits, single-file line
"Drop your clothes to the ground
turn and face us!"
the officer shouts over our heads

"Lift your nuts with one hand
sweep with the other
Open your mouth wide
pull your lips out

Turn around, face the wall, grab your toes
spread your cheeks, squat down
cough loud and hard
We have all day"

The guy next to me does not
he is handcuffed and carried away
Suddenly I'm reminded of my ex-girlfriend
enjoying life with a million new men

(those silent blood pumping beasts)
She is a baby maker of darkness
free on the streets, not taking my calls
The whore! The whore!

Bradley Brown

Hearing Voices

In a dimly lit cell
a man with a devil head over his heart
assembles a tool to draw blood from my body

His tattoos are free handed
from the imagination of a lifer
doing double L for triple M

I am out of my mind for most of every day
only traveling to the cafeteria, quick breakfast and dinner
with hundreds of men in yellow jumpsuits

We sit down, shout using spoons
while guards on catwalks with rifles orbit above
within range if not earshot

Call my sister from the only phone on the yard
We talk about her kids, the family
my new artist friend

Careful not to mention time, she asks if I'm all right
have her letters come through? I try to change the subject
watch what we say

"Person A is not speaking to Person B
Person C hasn't been seen in weeks
got caught using H on the job

Mom says you need someone
to cook and take care of you
Like a good Christian woman"

The recording reminds us we are being recorded
then an officer in the tower warns us
our time is almost up

Bradley Brown

Take Flight

The razor wire is so vibrant
you can hear it humming
like the coils of a toaster oven
angry with electricity

Ringing the prison
it lights up at sunset sometimes
Weak neon evenings
Sad, sad sign

Treble from metal speakers on wooden poles
announce "Yard is open. Yard is open"
Inmates in coats and skull caps
burst from buildings

Legions of men scream
take flight
Blue clad beings collide
and crash around

The one to be remembered
Record breaker people killer
Voices explode from every speaker
"GET DOWN! GET DOWN!"

Human sheaths wrap themselves around shanks
while skulls unlock under socks with rocks

Alarm bells peal and repeal out of unison
as high-powered rifles pop in sequence

When it stops I'm on the ground
on my back, spread eagle
puddling blood
shouts getting closer

Wince at the sky
stuck on the razor wire
is a bird leg without its body
Standing, like nothing happened

Bradley Brown

Tail of the Lizard King

On the floor of the throne room I awoke at dawn
strapped my boots on, fixed my hair to a radio song

It was a thousand years to the end of the day
I stared in the mirror, practiced what to say

What was reflected did not blink
seemed without reason and unable to think

Several warm beers were on the sink
from each one I took a drink

The queen's hideout was located at last
so continued my quest for another piece of ass

Tattoo Talk

He lifts his eyebrows politely and asks
in reference to my ink
"Why are they all about women?"

"What else is there to do?"
Reflect on the daughter of liberty
dancing above a hammer and sickle

her arms out, losing clothes
Martini glass in one hand
cigarette the other

Or the party girl gripping a chainsaw
cut-off jeans ripping into nowhere
body drawn back, full chested snarl

"My leg tattoos say it all" I continue
On the right calf, Frankenstein head
fixates on the left calf

where his bride's
blank expression stares back
"They can never actually kiss"

Skull and Crossbones

Bomb out of the supermarket pushing a shopping cart
smash it into the curb. Stand for the small photo
big booking number. Hold a sign and smile
my beer-run ends in a flash

Back on the streets within hours
I snatch a shoebox of mix tapes and phone numbers
get faded in a creepy neighborhood
and somehow bum a ride out

Our twisted smiles connect
walking stiff-legged along the pier
She takes me to the beach party with a buried keg
bonfire encampment amid crashing waves

Bound by determination and firm resolution
her fingers touch my six-pack
"Tomorrow, most decidedly
definitely tomorrow...

Tonight we rage
What's your poison?"
Boom box blowing my mind
smoke pours over us, twirls inland

Enter the Hero

(after school)
On the floor of her apartment
I shot heroin for the first time today
Bought the bag

begged a needle
had her do the rest
Blinked as the sky mooned me
cars honking

(date unknown)
If only I could get clean
or pure
needles and dope

(time of arrest)
Good evening, how may I help you?
You can start with the money in the register
including all big bills under the till

(mid-sentence)
Just thought I'd write to say
send money please
Love you

Bradley Brown

Heroin of the Story

I'm sitting with this junky, an older version of me
who is doing 25-to-life for a third strike
Armed robbery without ammo

When his first parole hearing starts nine thousand
one hundred and twenty-five days from now
a table of people will look to each other and say

"Nope... guns were used in every crime"
They will not know what's-his-name as I did
gentle, articulate, intelligent, taken by an addiction

He is without hope of release
unable to grasp the thought of his wife
or touch his true love on the streets

In Certain Cities

Many of these dogs will never
see the bare foot of a woman again
All they will know until their death
are men's faces, hands and genitalia

No panty hose or painted toes
just blue denim, dorky mustaches
dirty socks for lonely nights, dudes all around
For many weeks I considered this

little death: no more dainty feet
dancing off underwear after a midnight snack
No stockings, leggings, or lingerie
Not any kind ever again

Life without in a packed dormitory
no fireworks or explosions of the mind
Picture a sardine smoking a cigarette
by himself before bed, that was me

I may die unknown, unimportant
childish and childless
My life repossessed
Sucker karma collecting

Cast Her Crying Spell

I.
Nihilism dressed in long, black clothing
got caught smoking by a substitute
Got detention. His name was I

My new crush, the basket case with crazy eyes
tripped from the backseat of a Cadillac
spilling her bag on the curb

She bent over, mouth trembling
I saw the distinct outline
of animal jawbone

heard foul language
The smell of skunk weed
clenched my imagination

II.
A clock captivated the classroom
but for me it was about her. Sordid
fantasies snagged in casual glances

Detention let out
she was swept up
by an older guy in a hotrod

Alone, I walked into the grim field
behind the school

an enchanted sunset ablaze

Another blue and pink
disaster from above, pouring over
my trench coat of tears

Caterpillar Girl With Spider Legs

I crawled through her window for a quickie
It was a hundred hands, silky underwear
little else

Arrived numb, silent, salty-eyed
I fell with candy-cane wrists
that were wrapped and kissed

She fluttered about the room
from closet to dresser to drawer
changing into comfortable clothing

Then it was mouth to mouth
we were toe to toe, eye lashes touching
nothing missed

Pink webbed-stockings all over me
I recollect butterfly kisses
time on exquisite wings

Bad Memory

I listened to his war stories
while brushing my teeth, back turned
Could always feel his pain

They gave him 28 years with half-time
That was at least 5,267 days
to the free world

He turned himself in after graduation
day before 4th of July
no action, no appeal

"Back then the exercise yards had iron
and we watched TV all night
We used to own this place, did whatever

1984 took C-Files out of our hands
1994 gave us three strikes
and added more officers per bodies

Used to be murder to get life
now rats run the yard
Cops feed them cheeseburgers for telling"

I spat into the dim sink and looked up
at my reflection secured on the wall
in a small, square piece of metal

Bradley Brown

scratched by countless before me
How odd, I thought
enemies of the mirror

made a weapon and left a mark
Just like my cell mate
hating life and showing it

Magic Eight Ball, Magic Eight Ball

I.

After finishing a dime bag
the multiple personalities of a magnetic chick
told my fortune in the master bedroom

She was leaning against the headboard
a shoestring hung around her neck
its small noose knotted between her breast

A lighter flicked a couple failed attempts
a hand cupped its skinny flame
and she began talking

"Don't be so fiendlike or faithful
your girlfriend is in a bed right now
Horrorshow days ahead, very horrorshow

That one night stand from the orange groves
was looking for you. I sent her away
with something in hand

When things are dead outside
put a mirror under your nose
to see if you're alive

Do enough to remember
nothing of this conversation…"
She threw me a condom, closed the door

II.
We spent the afternoon at a restaurant
getting to know each other by studying
how other people order from the menu

"In this peculiar world of humans
it's a sobering experience to say
nothing is ever enough

Do I ramble on drugs?" she asked
smoking a cigarette with faraway eyes
like civilization was its ashes

Definitely talked on drugs
like too much coffee in the all-night diner
What's next? I said to the floor

"Can't predict now
ask again later. Try being a gentleman
and open the door"

Automatic Writing

I.

These poems that no one sees have always been here
like the odd infidelity that seems to occur around me

Wish it was easy as Russian roulette
putting pen to paper, catching you red-handed

My dream car rolling through the inky night
something caught in the headlights

Home early, the look on your face
worth a million words

II.

It is unseen that steals from my lungs
like powerful spirits taken back

Thoughts as heated arguments from a cold place
the blasts of breath slow to dissipate

It was a fallen flower, petal by petal that moved me
She loved me she loved me not

Saw the invisible lovers disrobe
saw right through their act (to write this)

Bradley Brown

Ghost Stories

Crazy... bummer... not cool...
Santa Cruz Sentinel
Man found dead inside Capitola residence

House of wild party
Too much tissue paper
another clogged toilet in the suburbs

Remembering the old bicycle haunts
I started to withdraw at night
Time-travel was hell

    ***

By and by skin popper
no ribbon of blood in the dropper
only abscessed veins and infected cavities

Went to score but got brought in
under intense fluorescent
smudged with ink

Graduated to orange pants
Drifted the dry plains painting the town
red. Scary places now and then

    ***

At the round table a group of strangers
claiming my blood fill their glasses
with juice from a machine

We wear our sorry stupid looking old clothes
and gather at one big stupid building
with lots of stupid people

This is how I think
the lonely drunk at 3:00 am
Die and walk a lonely earth

***

Float over couches and cushions upon waking
then ride to the costume party
for an unexpected appearance

Saturday night we toilet paper the campus
mummy-wrap its mascot and pose in character
hieroglyphs for the Polaroid

I slur something nasty like follow me
take your clothes off in bed. Let morning
pull the sheets over our heads

Bradley Brown

Horrorshow Days Ahead

I.
Supermarket weekday, weekend highway and shop
shambling parades, unreal, repeating
disappearing by evening...

Mindless wandering when the mall is opened, stammering
through doors and racks of clothes, struggling
without purpose through pockets and purses

I'm stuck in my body, transformed
at the liquor store buying a bag of food
Chips and soda, a cherry-flavored lollipop

II.
Crawl from some quiet mess on a master bed
and slam through doors to stagger to car
Sail against traffic past murmuring breakfast crowds

in sunglasses shining from tables along the boulevard
People cough and mutter to one another
as I turn the wheel, music blaring

Desolate scenes beyond the windshield
smoke pouring from the driver's side
Wonder how to escape today

Meet the Wolf Man

Cannot afford to take the day off and get loaded
buying wild women stiff drinks
or fine hors d'oeuvres

I spend lost weekends changing positions on the couch
running to the restroom during commercial breaks
or not moving except to scratch at my face

Something beneath my clothes
twitches to life. I beg to be
locked in a small room for the night

but come to in need of a shower
reeking of garlic fries, tasting of blood
underwear where my wallet should be

Suburban Death Curse

I disappeared
down some evening valley heavy with smog
for a TV dinner in the dead evening of winter

Thousands of nights in made-up worlds
on dirty sofas against unwashed walls
we drank with friends, lip-syncing to oldies

Quick to decide on junk food at the mall
we tossed bread crumbs in a remote park, getting high
Our country was still at war

Weekends without hurry or wake up calls
our shady Sunday hangovers
overcast on a blanket, people watching

The alarm clock woke me at 3 am
I grabbed my boots and bagged lunch
slept in the truck for an hour

At night the spinning doorway again
my bedroom window breaking
everyone eyeballing me

An episode of Twilight Zone
the drunk that won't go away
dinner in the freezer, burning

Another Visit

Shuddering prison bound bus
we are party animals shackled in pairs
in plastic chairs too small for grown men

We crouch in fetal seating positions
and freeze our asses off because (of course)
there is no heater on a prison bus

After delivery we bend over and cough
(the proverbial slap) as a man with authority
peers into lord knows what

What had the drugs undone?
How many women will not have sex with me now?
"The horror, the horror"

Then street lights flicker
two minutes after twelve
and teeth of a zipper pinch me

"Ever been to Omaha?"
she asks
taking off my blue jeans

"Don't Try"

I.
Coolest spot in town was the graveyard
where we got together
Far from high school
eternally spilling our guts
to each other

Tons of dirt between us

II.
Her diary said:
I finally got together with that guy in math
Nervous with rubber legs
learning to trust in me
he was too nice

I kill boys and birth men

III.
Hands scanning over her own belly
she felt for an ugly swelling
Nine months of nausea
poked a phantom finger
gagged her with a spoon

Mix of all flavors back again

IV.

Cryptic notes were passed at the blackboard
while rumors spread by touch
"She's turning into
a freak." Her favorite drink
was a mix of all flavors

Called it a suicide

V.
They found her body last night
skinny vessel, forever beautiful
floating in the icy mortuary
soon to be uncorked where it mattered most
Red Braille to be read

connecting the dots

VI.
Though it's almost a week after Valentine's day
bouquets still flower from headstones
A girl wearing a pink scarf and combat boots
stands up, looks over the lawn
catches my yawn

and winks

Auto Body

They found a suicide note under her pillow
with four songs she wanted to be played
at the cremation ceremony

Her parents won't let us talk
They said she hasn't been normal
since we met

My mom offered to rent me a limo for prom
but freaked when I said it should be a hearse
She just won't let go of the wheel, ha ha

Under restriction I sneak out
to a party where a bunch of girls are staying out late
One walks me home at 3am

We do our goodnight at my window
wasn't a real kiss but it was cool
Not long after that I lose it

O.D. on cold medicine
slash my wrists over love ballads
punch a wall, kick the television

They tell me to take down my posters
give me colorful pills that kill appetites
and bite on the brain like a zombie

My Girlfriend Was A Drug Dealer

Knock knock one cold foggy
to buy low-grade heroin, time out
and score some strange

My flesh shivered
the ache and arctic fever
only sold in black tar empires

"You're a selfish asshole"
she sighed out the window
offering me the works

Like a dull landing from ten stories, bones
had lingered twenty odd days waiting
Thick water little stabber, vacuum flower

Blood in blood out, the old in and out
like clockwork (or else)
Everything got much better (and worse)

"We're perfect for each other"
I said into the tiny plastic bag
"Will you always love me?"

Hurts to laugh because
many times I too said yes
to many things with many people

Bradley Brown

Dying For A Blast

From the window slat
I could see the flag
waving its arms

To get here we had toured the countryside
by bus ride past plants that produced steel
beyond the hills built by stars

Forward through small towns, behind billboard mermaids
to a sunset under sirens. The impossible city
its bomb proof boxes huddled in darkness

fed only by a lost highway
hidden by distance
Good times not up for grabs

Peon Poetry

Quit my paper route
to scoop bubblegum ice cream
Get giggles with bathroom humor
straws poking out my nose

Switch jobs to the Record Stop down the way
where I watch girls from the shoe shop
walk to and fro, stoop down from foot to foot
their loud miniskirts flashing across the mall

Then a breakfast diner has me do dishes
amid the stinky steam and greasy scraps
which I pick at and gobble down
Plunge toilets when necessary

A potato factory and liquor store
work me over sixty hours a week
Then my girlfriend starts cheating on me
horrifying tale I tell you

but choke from laughter on the porch with friends
next door a circus tent without doors. I pass out
in the bracelets of a waitress. In a used napkin
her number and lipstick kiss

Pick up the last check on Friday
ride towards Sunday, dreary Bloody Mary's

smiling at more opposite sex
Happy pissing my life away

I call a number off the wall
and keep to my circle of friends
quietly immersed in research
for our great American novel

The goal is to work as little as possible
smoke pot, drink until something comes up
take drugs, read books, watch movies
and listen to music while smoking more pot

Friends come over to buy bags of weed
complain about stupid questions
petty scandals around pretty co-workers
white collar crime, its blue collar blood

My future as a young man
washing up from time to time
Call in sick when things get dirty
Hit the joint, write to get clean

American Standard

Fun forever and ever hallelujah amen
I ran to the next party
and the party after that
I had to, my drink needed a drink

Friends of the parking lot
do you remember our cry from the wilderness?
Bookending normal life
our relegated prayers from the wasteland?

Water never fell out of the blue
instead it rained satellite feed
sunburn
and static

Hitched our station wagons behind falling stars
to a giant lake in the sky, where we
cast our poles into the wished-for...
Went overboard when it was time to go

I'm sure you have no idea
what I'm talking about
Don't worry, be good (or bad)
someday you may

The clock reads 13:00
it is a bright hot day in September

Bradley Brown

Distracted by lonely spirits
life is behind numbered doors

I am born again above the throne
given a second chance
razor wire for a crown
warehouse for a home

Blues In Drag

Collect call from a California state prison
"Are the stories of soap in the shower...?"
Interrupting I assure her that doesn't happen (often)

Don't bother mentioning the wet sounds in the shower room
tobacco pulled from an ass, then paper and lighter
or blood streaming from fingers around a neck

If I keep my mouth shut
things will get better
That was the truth

"Must confess
I have high spirits
and very clean, promise

Exercising, muscles gaining mass
gradually strengthening
remarkably happy..."

Fell Through

To our father
who is not
in hell

He ate the cookies
left a crumby plate
drank milk from a half empty cup

While we hid listening, covered
in quilted blankets, he shook
the reindeer bells and stomped over head

But winter is forgetful
misplacing good dads
husbandry in its hoary wake

I saw something on a blank page
footprints trailing into the blizzard
If heaven froze over

our father would
write his name in the snow
go ice-fishing on the lake with fire

Beach Cruiser

"Welcome to shit world
Blame is a flame and
I burn with liquid"

says the scary haircut with no hands
as it rides up and down the coast
dodging police cars. That is

until armored motorcades locate him
at a punishing drive-thru neighborhood
near the shores of southern California

It's back to the old house again
Bicycle take down, no shoes or shirt
hands in the air

Spokes of a wheel stop
spikes of a mohawk
roll in the sand

Inland Empire

Regardless of who or what
I never feel completely human
unless there is a woman above me

like something out of a movie...
Down dark hallways to a warm vestibule
the hand-held mirror and her thin smoke...

We share the infamous cigarette after
while the world sleeps through the years
It's a haunted screenplay about

some sick nightmare playing the part
opposite the lady standing alone
We bounce on a bed together

I leave through the window in the wee hours
Part of me is that punk rocker, party crasher
who lives on his back and is dying to escape

Out there in the ocean of lights on the desert floor
he turns up at serious or slow moments
and almost ruins the film every time

Cell #237

Blacking out in the whiteout hotel
Jack tried being Henry, writing
the great American novel drunk

Unbeknownst to his fake wife
he mixed with former guests and caretakers
at the ghastly bar overlooking a fantastic ballroom

He got furious with the typewriter
trying on that cabin fever feeling
Then chopped at it with a fire ax

"Where are the girls?" was his only poem
It said the same phrase on hundreds of pages
"All work and no play makes me a bad, bad boy"

Bradley Brown

Possessions

I.
Can't count how many times we were counted
got on the ground or passed through check points
Can't tell how many times we were told on

bunks tossed, lockers stripped
Overcrowded and loud, everyone watching
incarceration was possessionless and sad

Wrote letters to loved ones on weekends
strung laundry outside on the yard
keeping an eye on my underwear

Everything on my person at time of arrest
will be returned upon departure
I can change from who I was into clean clothes

swagger out of this state washing machine
head south, score at the first stop
meet her at some dirty meat market

By the time you read this we'll be long gone
enjoying the flesh as usual, but I'll marry
a respectable woman and settle down soon

II.
Get to the parole office
was the only requirement of release

I had 48 hours to make a masterpiece

Just like the game of Monopoly
nowhere to live, zero people to see
nothing to do but dwindle $200 gate money

Encounter the love of my life
buy chance at some roadhouse
take a drink, leave the body

Cheers to being a decent human in the future
summer dresses pound the pavement
Hollywood at sunset, fit for consumption

So this smoking hot chick walks into a bar
orders something made-up, turns and says
"Want to see the world with me?"

No matter what bartender we ordered from
I'll be damned, there we were
nothing in our hands

Bradley Brown

Exorcism of Inmate P33750

I.

At a state correctional facility
during another lockdown status
(no program, no dayroom, no yard)

an all-night party came to me
Year of graduation, mountain town
full of actors

pretending to be movie stars
She drove us up to Idyllwild one Saturday
in the refracted sunlight of that first summer

Loose asphalt roads hidden beside
roof stones angled in the upsweep of arboriculture
outcroppings of rock, pine, and pointed cabin

We hiked around a clearing
guarded by needled trees turned totem poles
carved from the terrible teeth of chainsaws

High at the base of a great granite peak, manics
looked into the monstrous face of Tahquitz
the suicide king, before descending

Last visage wasted on the valley far below
sprawling shimmering, down into
the unfathomable evening

Boy and girl walking a distant road
in the height of fashion at the end of night
Songs on the radio, one shadow growing

II.
Fast forward: big house blues
Want to rush the exit, beat the traffic
like a crowd after the performance

Or a group of demons fleeing
a truly horrible mind...
There are worse places

That first set of lights...
the high school where I grew up
Built on the site of a condemned playhouse

I remember reading a history book
from the future. Anecdotal daydreams
like chalk dust from the drawing board

It is very important to say that
I was not in love with her
I only loved her

Somewhere there's a female
on a mattress yelling obscenities
wanting to do things no one has done before

Boy meets girl again and again
double vision times deja vu
Until it's written in stone "c'est la vie"

Father, give me a cigarette
and please something to drink
Make it holy water for my hangover

THANK YOU

Brad Brown
San Diego, California
2019

Made in the USA
San Bernardino, CA
19 March 2019

One collection like one poem. Outside of geography

found writings of self discovery and other cheesy pastimes

Grab something to drink, find somewhere quiet

Please read aloud, from Alpha to Omega

Thought it'd be published posthumously

Cheers to winning

Lion's blood

drink up to get down

Half smiling

half drowning

"The Humble Narrator"

Bradley Brown

Inland Empire is the author's second book of poetry. He is currently working on three projects: a novel, an instruction manual, and another book of poems. Bradley enjoys outdoor activities, downhill skateboarding and walking in city parks.
He is a mathematician by day and serious writer at night. His favorite water is clean.

B07PPQ7WRM